WELCOME TO THE BATHROOM.

IF YOU HAVEN'T ALREADY PLEASE SEAT YOURSELF. WHEN COMFORTABLE, SIGN IN AND ANSWER THE QUESTION.

WE ASK THAT YOU URINATE WITH PRECISION AND ELEGANCE.

REMEMBER SPRINKLES ARE FOR CUPCAKES AND TOILET SEATS

Before you sign in please answer!

THE GREAT DEBATE

Please draw a little poop in the box you believe to be correct & write your name next to it.

Fig. 1.

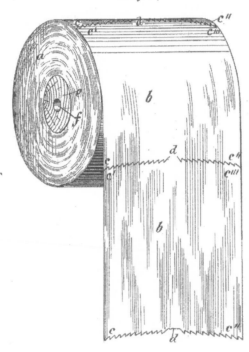

Fig. 2.

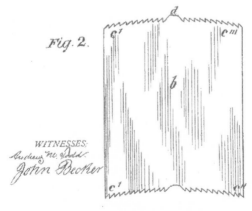

WITNESSES:

Andrew M. Dodd.

John Becker

INVENTOR,

Seth Wheeler.

DATE: ....

NAME: ....

REASON FOR VISIT: ....

Q Given The Choice Of Anyone In The World, Who Would
You Want As A Dinner Guest?

....
....
....
....
....
....

RATING 💩 💩 💩 💩 💩

DATE: ....

NAME: ....

REASON FOR VISIT: ....

Q Would You Like To Be Famous? In What Way?

....
....
....
....
....
....

RATING 🧻 🧻 🧻 🧻 🧻

DATE: ....

NAME: ....

REASON FOR VISIT: ....

Q Which Is The Most Beautiful Place In The World?

....
....
....
....
....
....

RATING 🧻 🧻 🧻 🧻 🧻

DATE: ....

NAME: ....

REASON FOR VISIT: ....

Q In One or 2 Sentences, Who Are You?

....
....
....
....
....
....

RATING 💩 💩 💩 💩 💩

DATE: ....

NAME: ....

REASON FOR VISIT: ....

Q Do you believe there is good in everyone?

....

....

....

....

....

....

RATING 💩 💩 💩 💩 💩

DATE: ....

NAME: ....

REASON FOR VISIT: ....

Q What part of a kid's movie completely scarred you?

....

....

....

....

....

....

RATING 🧻 🧻 🧻 🧻 🧻

DATE: ....

NAME: ....

REASON FOR VISIT: ....

Q What kind of secret society would you like to start?

....

....

....

....

....

....

RATING 🧻 🧻 🧻 🧻 🧻

DATE: ....

NAME: ....

REASON FOR VISIT: ....

Q What Do You Think Is The Most Significant Event In The History Of Humans?

....

....

....

....

....

RATING 💩 💩 💩 💩 💩

DATE: ....

NAME: ....

REASON FOR VISIT: ....

Q What's the most ridiculous fact you know? ...

....

....

....

....

....

....

RATING 💩💩💩💩💩

DATE: ....

NAME: ....

REASON FOR VISIT: ....

Q What is the funniest joke you know by heart? ...

....

....

....

....

....

....

RATING 🧻🧻🧻🧻🧻

DATE: ....

NAME: ....

REASON FOR VISIT: ....

Q In 44 years, what will people be nostalgic for? ...

....

....

....

....

....

....

RATING 🧻🧻🧻🧻🧻

DATE: ....

NAME: ....

REASON FOR VISIT: ....

Q What are the unwritten rules of where you work? ...

....

....

....

....

....

....

RATING 💩💩💩💩💩

DATE: ....
NAME: ....
REASON FOR VISIT: ....
Q What's The 1 Thing You Wish To Accomplish Before
You Die? ....
....
....
....
....
....
....
RATING 💩💩💩💩💩

DATE: ....
NAME: ....
REASON FOR VISIT: ....
Q What's Something You Think Every Person Should
Experience In Their Lifetime? ....
....
....
....
....
....
....
RATING 🧻🧻🧻🧻🧻

DATE: ....
NAME: ....
REASON FOR VISIT: ....
Q What's The Wisest Thing You Have Ever Heard
Someone Say? ....
....
....
....
....
....
....
RATING 🧻🧻🧻🧻🧻

DATE: ....
NAME: ....
REASON FOR VISIT: ....
Q What Is Your Life Story? (in brief)
....
....
....
....
....
....
....
RATING 💩💩💩💩💩

DATE: ....
NAME: ....
REASON FOR VISIT: ....
Q In one or two sentences, how would you sum up the
internet? ....
....
....
....
....
....
RATING 💩 💩 💩 💩 💩

DATE: ....
NAME: ....
REASON FOR VISIT: ....
Q What's the most imaginative insult you can come
up with? ....
....
....
....
....
....
RATING 🧻 🧻 🧻 🧻 🧻

DATE: ....
NAME: ....
REASON FOR VISIT: ....
Q What mythical creature would improve the world
most if it existed? ....
....
....
....
....
....
RATING 🧻 🧻 🧻 🧻 🧻

DATE: ....
NAME: ....
REASON FOR VISIT: ....
Q What Could You Pay More Attention To In Life?
....
....
....
....
....
....
RATING 💩 💩 💩 💩 💩

DATE: ....

NAME: ....

REASON FOR VISIT: ....

Q What secret conspiracy would you like to start?

....
....
....
....
....
....
....

RATING 💩💩💩💩💩

DATE: ....

NAME: ....

REASON FOR VISIT: ....

Q What are your thoughts on trump?

....
....
....
....
....
....

RATING 🧻🧻🧻🧻🧻

DATE: ....

NAME: ....

REASON FOR VISIT: ....

Q What's invisible but you wish people could see?

....
....
....
....
....
....

RATING 🧻🧻🧻🧻🧻

DATE: ....

NAME: ....

REASON FOR VISIT: ....

Q What's the weirdest thing you have ever smelt?

....
....
....
....
....

RATING 💩💩💩💩💩

DATE: ....

NAME: ....

REASON FOR VISIT: ....

Q If Your Life Was A Movie, What Would The Title Be?

....
....
....
....
....
....
....

RATING 💩 💩 💩 💩 💩

DATE: ....

NAME: ....

REASON FOR VISIT: ....

Q What is the funniest joke you know by heart?

....
....
....
....
....
....
....

RATING 🧻 🧻 🧻 🧻 🧻

DATE: ....

NAME: ....

REASON FOR VISIT: ....

Q What would be the creepiest thing you could say while passing a stranger on the street? ....

....
....
....
....
....
....

RATING 🧻 🧻 🧻 🧻 🧻

DATE: ....

NAME: ....

REASON FOR VISIT: ....

Q If You Had To Work But Didn't Need The Money, What Would You Choose To Do? ....

....
....
....
....
....
....

RATING 💩 💩 💩 💩 💩

DATE: ....

NAME: ....

REASON FOR VISIT: ....

Q If You Could Dis-Invent One Thing, What Would It Be?

....

....

....

....

....

....

RATING 💩 💩 💩 💩 💩

DATE: ....

NAME: ....

REASON FOR VISIT: ....

Q What is the best quote you know by heart?

....

....

....

....

....

....

RATING

DATE: ....

NAME: ....

REASON FOR VISIT: ....

Q What is the best chat up line?

....

....

....

....

....

....

RATING

DATE: ....

NAME: ....

REASON FOR VISIT: ....

Q What are the unwritten rules of your relationship?

....

....

....

....

....

RATING 💩 💩 💩 💩 💩

DATE: ....

NAME: ....

REASON FOR VISIT: ....

Q Is free will real or just an illusion? ....

....

....

....

....

....

RATING 💩💩💩💩💩

DATE: ....

NAME: ....

REASON FOR VISIT: ....

Q Is there a meaning to life? If so, what is it? ..

....

....

....

....

....

RATING 🧻🧻🧻🧻🧻

DATE: ....

NAME: ....

REASON FOR VISIT: ....

Q Do you believe in God? Explain ....

....

....

....

....

....

RATING 🧻🧻🧻🧻🧻

DATE: ....

NAME: ....

REASON FOR VISIT: ....

Q Why do we dream? ....

....

....

....

....

....

RATING 💩💩💩💩💩

DATE: ....

NAME: ....

REASON FOR VISIT: ....

Q What do you remember most from school?
....
....
....
....
....
....
....

RATING 💩💩💩💩💩

DATE: ....

NAME: ....

REASON FOR VISIT: ....

Q What is the best and worst purchases you've ever made?
....
....
....
....
....
....

RATING 🧻🧻🧻🧻🧻

DATE: ....

NAME: ....

REASON FOR VISIT: ....

Q What is something that is trendy now, but in 5 years everyone will look back on and be embarrassed by?
....
....
....
....
....
....

RATING 🧻🧻🧻🧻🧻

DATE: ....

NAME: ....

REASON FOR VISIT: ....

Q What accomplishment are you most proud of?
....
....
....
....
....

RATING 💩💩💩💩💩

DATE: ....

NAME: ....

REASON FOR VISIT: ....

Q How will humans as a species go extinct? ....

....

....

....

....

....

....

RATING 💩💩💩💩💩

DATE: ....

NAME: ....

REASON FOR VISIT: ....

Q What are some interesting alternatives to war that countries could settle their differences with? ......

....

....

....

....

....

....

RATING 🧻🧻🧻🧻🧻

DATE: ....

NAME: ....

REASON FOR VISIT: ....

Q What do you think would be humanity's reaction to the discovery of extraterrestrial life? ....

....

....

....

....

....

....

RATING 🧻🧻🧻🧻🧻

DATE: ....

NAME: ....

REASON FOR VISIT: ....

Q If you were arrested with no explanation, what would your friends and family assume you had done? ....

....

....

....

....

....

....

RATING 💩💩💩💩💩

DATE: ....

NAME: ....

REASON FOR VISIT: ....

Q You're a mad scientist, what scientific experiment would you run if money and ethics weren't an issue?

....

....

....

....

....

....

....

RATING 💩 💩 💩 💩 💩

DATE: ....

NAME: ....

REASON FOR VISIT: ....

Q What is the funniest joke you know by heart?

....

....

....

....

....

....

....

RATING 🧻 🧻 🧻 🧻 🧻

DATE: ....

NAME: ....

REASON FOR VISIT: ....

Q What Lessons In Life Did You Learn To Hard Way?

....

....

....

....

....

....

....

RATING 🧻 🧻 🧻 🧻 🧻

DATE: ....

NAME: ....

REASON FOR VISIT: ....

Q If You Could Be A Member Of Any Tv-Sitcom Family, Which Would It Be?

....

....

....

....

....

....

....

RATING 💩 💩 💩 💩 💩

DATE: ....

NAME: ....

REASON FOR VISIT: ....

Q Will religion ever become obsolete? ....

....

....

....

....

....

....

....

RATING 💩 💩 💩 💩 💩

DATE: ....

NAME: ....

REASON FOR VISIT: ....

Q What are some fun ways to answer everyday questions like "how' are you" or "what do you do"?

....

....

....

....

....

....

....

RATING 🧻 🧻 🧻 🧻 🧻

DATE: ....

NAME: ....

REASON FOR VISIT: ....

Q Do You Think It's Too Late To Do Certain Things In Your Life? Why?

....

....

....

....

....

....

RATING 🧻 🧻 🧻 🧻 🧻

DATE: ....

NAME: ....

REASON FOR VISIT: ....

Q How do you think your future self will remember your current self??

....

....

....

....

....

....

RATING 💩 💩 💩 💩 💩

DATE: ....

NAME: ....

REASON FOR VISIT: ....

Q What's the most weirdest thing you have seen in someones bathroom? (apart from this book) ....

....

....

....

....

....

....

....

RATING 💩 💩 💩 💩 💩

DATE: ....

NAME: ....

REASON FOR VISIT: ....

Q What is the funniest joke you know by heart?

....

....

....

....

....

....

....

RATING 🧻 🧻 🧻 🧻 🧻

DATE: ....

NAME: ....

REASON FOR VISIT: ....

Q Where 's the most beautiful place you've ever been?

....

....

....

....

....

....

....

RATING 🧻 🧻 🧻 🧻 🧻

DATE: ....

NAME: ....

REASON FOR VISIT: ....

Q What are your 3 favorite movies?

....

....

....

....

....

....

....

RATING 💩 💩 💩 💩 💩

DATE: ....

NAME: ....

REASON FOR VISIT: ....

Q What's the right age to get married? ....

....

....

....

....

....

RATING 💩 💩 💩 💩 💩

DATE: ....

NAME: ....

REASON FOR VISIT: ....

Q If you were transported 500 years into the past with nothing, how would you prove that you were from the future?

....

....

....

....

RATING 🧻 🧻 🧻 🧻 🧻

DATE: ....

NAME: ....

REASON FOR VISIT: ....

Q If you could have dinner with anyone from history, who would it be? ....

....

....

....

....

....

RATING 🧻 🧻 🧻 🧻 🧻

DATE: ....

NAME: ....

REASON FOR VISIT: ....

Q If you could know the absolute and total truth to one question, what question would you ask? ....

....

....

....

....

RATING 💩 💩 💩 💩 💩

DATE: ....

NAME: ....

REASON FOR VISIT: ....

Q What's the most interesting thing you've read or seen this week??

....

....

....

....

....

....

RATING 💩💩💩💩💩

DATE: ....

NAME: ....

REASON FOR VISIT: ....

Q What's the most useless talent you have?

....

....

....

....

....

....

....

RATING 🧻🧻🧻🧻🧻

DATE: ....

NAME: ....

REASON FOR VISIT: ....

Q If you were wrongfully put into an asylum, how would you convince them that you're actually sane and not just pretending to be sane?

....

....

....

....

....

....

RATING 🧻🧻🧻🧻🧻

DATE: ....

NAME: ....

REASON FOR VISIT: ....

Q If someone asked to be your apprentice and learn all that you know, what would you teach them??

....

....

....

....

....

....

RATING 💩💩💩💩💩

DATE: ....

NAME: ....

REASON FOR VISIT: ....

Q Who are the 3 greatest living musicians? ....

....

....

....

....

....

....

RATING 💩 💩 💩 💩 💩

DATE: ....

NAME: ....

REASON FOR VISIT: ....

Q Who would play you in a movie of your life? And why? ..

....

....

....

....

....

....

RATING 🧻 🧻 🧻 🧻 🧻

DATE: ....

NAME: ....

REASON FOR VISIT: ....

Q In 44 years, what will people be nostalgic for? ......

....

....

....

....

....

....

RATING 🧻 🧻 🧻 🧻 🧻

DATE: ....

NAME: ....

REASON FOR VISIT: ....

Q If you won the lottery what would you do? ...

....

....

....

....

....

....

RATING 💩 💩 💩 💩 💩

DATE: ....

NAME: ....

REASON FOR VISIT: ....

Q What are some things that sound like compliments but are actually insults?? ....

....
....
....
....
....
....

RATING 💩💩💩💩💩

DATE: ....

NAME: ....

REASON FOR VISIT: ....

Q What is the most embarrassing way you've been injured? ....

....
....
....
....
....
....

RATING 🧻🧻🧻🧻🧻

DATE: ....

NAME: ....

REASON FOR VISIT: ....

Q When was the last time you tried something new? ....

....
....
....
....
....
....

RATING 🧻🧻🧻🧻🧻

DATE: ....

NAME: ....

REASON FOR VISIT: ....

Q Who do you sometimes compare yourself to? ....

....
....
....
....
....
....

RATING 💩💩💩💩💩

DATE: ....

NAME: ....

REASON FOR VISIT: ....

Q What life lesson did you learn the hard way? ....

....

....

....

....

....

....

RATING 💩 💩 💩 💩 💩

DATE: ....

NAME: ....

REASON FOR VISIT: ....

Q What do you wish you spent more time doing five years ago? ....

....

....

....

....

....

....

RATING 🧻 🧻 🧻 🧻 🧻

DATE: ....

NAME: ....

REASON FOR VISIT: ....

Q IWhat would you do differently if you knew nobody would judge you? ....

....

....

....

....

....

....

RATING 🧻 🧻 🧻 🧻 🧻

DATE: ....

NAME: ....

REASON FOR VISIT: ....

Q What is the difference between living and existing? ....

....

....

....

....

....

....

RATING 💩 💩 💩 💩 💩

DATE: ....

NAME: ....

REASON FOR VISIT: ....

Q Have you done anything lately worth remembering?

....

....

....

....

....

....

RATING 💩💩💩💩💩

DATE: ....

NAME: ....

REASON FOR VISIT: ....

Q Which activities make you lose track of time?

....

....

....

....

....

....

RATING 🧻🧻🧻🧻🧻

DATE: ....

NAME: ....

REASON FOR VISIT: ....

Q Are you holding onto something that you need to let go of?

....

....

....

....

....

RATING 🧻🧻🧻🧻🧻

DATE: ....

NAME: ....

REASON FOR VISIT: ....

Q When you hit 80, what will matter to you the most?

....

....

....

....

....

RATING 💩💩💩💩💩

DATE: ....

NAME: ....

REASON FOR VISIT: ....

Q What makes you smile?

....

....

....

....

....

RATING 💩 💩 💩 💩 💩

DATE: ....

NAME: ....

REASON FOR VISIT: ....

Q If the average lifespan was only 41 years, how would you live your life differently? ....

....

....

....

....

....

RATING 🧻 🧻 🧻 🧻 🧻

DATE: ....

NAME: ....

REASON FOR VISIT: ....

Q What book would you choose as a mandatory read for all high school students and why? ....

....

....

....

....

....

RATING 🧻 🧻 🧻 🧻 🧻

DATE: ....

NAME: ....

REASON FOR VISIT: ....

Q What is important enough to go to war for?

....

....

....

....

....

RATING 💩 💩 💩 💩 💩

DATE: ....
NAME: ....
REASON FOR VISIT: ....
Q What are some desirable traits another person can possess? ....
....
....
....
....
....
....
RATING 💩💩💩💩💩

DATE: ....
NAME: ....
REASON FOR VISIT: ....
Q Is stealing to feed a starving child okay? Explain.
....
....
....
....
....
....
....
RATING 🧻🧻🧻🧻🧻

DATE: ....
NAME: ....
REASON FOR VISIT: ....
Q What do you want most?
....
....
....
....
....
....
....
RATING 🧻🧻🧻🧻🧻

DATE: ....
NAME: ....
REASON FOR VISIT: ....
Q If you could choose one thing to change in this world what would it be? ....
....
....
....
....
....
RATING 💩💩💩💩💩

DATE: ....

NAME: ....

REASON FOR VISIT: ....

Q If you have 3 wishes, what would they be? ...

....

....

....

....

....

....

RATING 💩💩💩💩💩

DATE: ....

NAME: ....

REASON FOR VISIT: ....

Q Can you describe your life in 2 sentences? ...

....

....

....

....

....

....

RATING 🧻🧻🧻🧻🧻

DATE: ....

NAME: ....

REASON FOR VISIT: ....

Q Is legacy important? ...

....

....

....

....

....

....

RATING 🧻🧻🧻🧻🧻

DATE: ....

NAME: ....

REASON FOR VISIT: ....

Q What has been the most defining point of your life so far? ...

....

....

....

....

....

....

RATING 💩💩💩💩💩

DATE: ....

NAME: ....

REASON FOR VISIT: ....

Q What lifts your spirits when times are tough?

....

....

....

....

....

....

....

RATING 💩 💩 💩 💩 💩

DATE: ....

NAME: ....

REASON FOR VISIT: ....

Q What is the funniest joke you know by heart?

....

....

....

....

....

....

....

RATING 🧻 🧻 🧻 🧻 🧻

DATE: ....

NAME: ....

REASON FOR VISIT: ....

Q What is your most beloved memory from childhood?

....

....

....

....

....

....

....

RATING 🧻 🧻 🧻 🧻 🧻

DATE: ....

NAME: ....

REASON FOR VISIT: ....

Q If you had the chance to go back in time and change 1 thing, what would it be & would you do it?

....

....

....

....

....

....

RATING 💩 💩 💩 💩 💩

DATE: ....

NAME: ....

REASON FOR VISIT: ....

Q If you were given only 5 years to live, what would you do with those years? ....

....

....

....

....

....

....

RATING 💩 💩 💩 💩 💩

DATE: ....

NAME: ....

REASON FOR VISIT: ....

Q What gives your life meaning?

....

....

....

....

....

....

RATING 🧻 🧻 🧻 🧻 🧻

DATE: ....

NAME: ....

REASON FOR VISIT: ....

Q What would you want people to remember you for after you have gone? ....

....

....

....

....

....

....

RATING 🧻 🧻 🧻 🧻 🧻

DATE: ....

NAME: ....

REASON FOR VISIT: ....

Q Do you believe in fate? Explain.

....

....

....

....

....

....

RATING 💩 💩 💩 💩 💩

DATE: ....

NAME: ....

REASON FOR VISIT: ....

Q What do you think you will be doing in 10 years time?

....

....

....

....

....

....

RATING 💩 💩 💩 💩 💩

DATE: ....

NAME: ....

REASON FOR VISIT: ....

Q What one small act of kindness will you never forget?

....

....

....

....

....

....

RATING 🧻 🧻 🧻 🧻 🧻

DATE: ....

NAME: ....

REASON FOR VISIT: ....

Q Would you rather lose all your old memories or never be able to make new ones?

....

....

....

....

....

....

RATING 🧻 🧻 🧻 🧻 🧻

DATE: ....

NAME: ....

REASON FOR VISIT: ....

Q What do you have that you can not live without?

....

....

....

....

....

....

RATING 💩 💩 💩 💩 💩

DATE: ....

NAME: ....

REASON FOR VISIT: ....

Q 5 words that describe the last 4 months of your life.

....
....
....
....
....

RATING 💩 💩 💩 💩 💩

DATE: ....

NAME: ....

REASON FOR VISIT: ....

Q What does freedom mean to you?

....
....
....
....
....

RATING 🧻 🧻 🧻 🧻 🧻

DATE: ....

NAME: ....

REASON FOR VISIT: ....

Q If happiness was the only currency, what would make you rich?

....
....
....
....
....

RATING 🧻 🧻 🧻 🧻 🧻

DATE: ....

NAME: ....

REASON FOR VISIT: ....

Q What are 3 moral rules that you would never break in your life?

....
....
....
....
....

RATING 💩 💩 💩 💩 💩

DATE: ....

NAME: ....

REASON FOR VISIT: ....

Q What would you not give up for 1 million in cash?
....
....
....
....
....
....

RATING 💩💩💩💩💩

DATE: ....

NAME: ....

REASON FOR VISIT: ....

Q When do you feel most like your true self?
....
....
....
....
....
....

RATING 🧻🧻🧻🧻🧻

DATE: ....

NAME: ....

REASON FOR VISIT: ....

Q If you could live one day in your life over again, what
   would it be? ....
....
....
....
....
....

RATING 🧻🧻🧻🧻🧻

DATE: ....

NAME: ....

REASON FOR VISIT: ....

Q How have you changed in the last 5 years?
....
....
....
....
....
....

RATING 💩💩💩💩💩

DATE: ....

NAME: ....

REASON FOR VISIT: ....

Q What's the most ridiculous fact you know?

....

....

....

....

....

RATING 💩 💩 💩 💩 💩

DATE: ....

NAME: ....

REASON FOR VISIT: ....

Q What is the funniest joke you know by heart?

....

....

....

....

....

RATING 🧻 🧻 🧻 🧻 🧻

DATE: ....

NAME: ....

REASON FOR VISIT: ....

Q What are you sure about in your life?

....

....

....

....

....

RATING 🧻 🧻 🧻 🧻 🧻

DATE: ....

NAME: ....

REASON FOR VISIT: ....

Q What is your definition of "heaven"?

....

....

....

....

....

RATING 💩 💩 💩 💩 💩

DATE: ....
NAME: ....
REASON FOR VISIT: ....
Q What makes someone beautiful?
....
....
....
....
....
....
RATING 💩💩💩💩💩

DATE: ....
NAME: ....
REASON FOR VISIT: ....
Q What is the funniest joke you know by heart?
....
....
....
....
....
....
RATING 🧻🧻🧻🧻🧻

DATE: ....
NAME: ....
REASON FOR VISIT: ....
Q In 44 years, what will people be nostalgic for?
....
....
....
....
....
....
RATING 🧻🧻🧻🧻🧻

DATE: ....
NAME: ....
REASON FOR VISIT: ....
Q What would you do if you accidentally killed someone?
....
....
....
....
....
....
RATING 💩💩💩💩💩

DATE: ....

NAME: ....

REASON FOR VISIT: ....

Q There is a fire, you can only save 1 bag of stuff, what would you put in there? ....

....

....

....

....

....

RATING 💩 💩 💩 💩 💩

DATE: ....

NAME: ....

REASON FOR VISIT: ....

Q If today was your last day, who would you call & what would you say? ....

....

....

....

....

....

RATING 🧻 🧻 🧻 🧻 🧻

DATE: ....

NAME: ....

REASON FOR VISIT: ....

Q If you could take one picture of your life, what would it look like? ....

....

....

....

....

....

RATING 🧻 🧻 🧻 🧻 🧻

DATE: ....

NAME: ....

REASON FOR VISIT: ....

Q What is the number one thing you need to accomplish before you die? ....

....

....

....

....

....

RATING 💩 💩 💩 💩 💩

DATE: ....

NAME: ....

REASON FOR VISIT: ....

Q Who is the strongest person you know and why? .....

....

....

....

....

....

RATING 💩💩💩💩💩

DATE: ....

NAME: ....

REASON FOR VISIT: ....

Q What is the funniest joke you know by heart? .....

....

....

....

....

....

RATING 🧻🧻🧻🧻🧻

DATE: ....

NAME: ....

REASON FOR VISIT: ....

Q What is your favorite song and why? .....

....

....

....

....

....

RATING 🧻🧻🧻🧻🧻

DATE: ....

NAME: ....

REASON FOR VISIT: ....

Q What is one thing that makes you really angry & why?

....

....

....

....

....

RATING 💩💩💩💩💩

DATE: ....

NAME: ....

REASON FOR VISIT: ....

Q Describe what love feels like. ....
....
....
....
....
....
....
....

RATING 💩💩💩💩💩

DATE: ....

NAME: ....

REASON FOR VISIT: ....

Q What is your earliest memory? ....
....
....
....
....
....
....
....

RATING 🧻🧻🧻🧻🧻

DATE: ....

NAME: ....

REASON FOR VISIT: ....

Q What book/film/music has had the greatest impact
on your life? ....
....
....
....
....
....
....

RATING 🧻🧻🧻🧻🧻

DATE: ....

NAME: ....

REASON FOR VISIT: ....

Q What 2 questions do you really want to know the
answers to? ....
....
....
....
....
....
....

RATING 💩💩💩💩💩

DATE: ....

NAME: ....

REASON FOR VISIT: ....

Q What's are you most looking forward to this month?

....

....

....

....

....

....

RATING 💩💩💩💩💩

DATE: ....

NAME: ....

REASON FOR VISIT: ....

Q What is one thing most people don't know about you?

....

....

....

....

....

....

RATING 🧻🧻🧻🧻🧻

DATE: ....

NAME: ....

REASON FOR VISIT: ....

Q If you could relive yesterday, would you do anything different? ....

....

....

....

....

....

RATING 🧻🧻🧻🧻🧻

DATE: ....

NAME: ....

REASON FOR VISIT: ....

Q Who is your role model and why?

....

....

....

....

....

....

RATING 💩💩💩💩💩

DATE: ....

NAME: ....

REASON FOR VISIT: ....

Q What has been on your mind the most this week?

....

....

....

....

....

RATING 💩 💩 💩 💩 💩

DATE: ....

NAME: ....

REASON FOR VISIT: ....

Q Where else in the world would you live and where?

....

....

....

....

....

RATING 🧻 🧻 🧻 🧻 🧻

DATE: ....

NAME: ....

REASON FOR VISIT: ....

Q What is your greatest strength & your main weakness?

....

....

....

....

....

RATING 🧻 🧻 🧻 🧻 🧻

DATE: ....

NAME: ....

REASON FOR VISIT: ....

Q What was the last thing you got angry about?

....

....

....

....

....

RATING 💩 💩 💩 💩 💩

DATE: ....

NAME: ....

REASON FOR VISIT: ....

Q What is the one thing you miss from the past & why?

....
....
....
....
....
....

RATING 💩💩💩💩💩

DATE: ....

NAME: ....

REASON FOR VISIT: ....

Q What is the weirdest thing you have ever done?

....
....
....
....
....
....

RATING 🧻🧻🧻🧻🧻

DATE: ....

NAME: ....

REASON FOR VISIT: ....

Q Describe the city/town where you live, what is the best thing and the worst?

....
....
....
....
....
....

RATING 🧻🧻🧻🧻🧻

DATE: ....

NAME: ....

REASON FOR VISIT: ....

Q What are the best ways to relax?

....
....
....
....
....
....

RATING 💩💩💩💩💩

DATE: ....

NAME: ....

REASON FOR VISIT: ....

Q What was the last white lie you told and to who?

....

....

....

....

....

....

RATING 💩💩💩💩💩

DATE: ....

NAME: ....

REASON FOR VISIT: ....

Q What is your ideal day?

....

....

....

....

....

....

RATING 🧻🧻🧻🧻🧻

DATE: ....

NAME: ....

REASON FOR VISIT: ....

Q If you could be a famous person for the day, who would you be and why?

....

....

....

....

....

RATING 🧻🧻🧻🧻🧻

DATE: ....

NAME: ....

REASON FOR VISIT: ....

Q What do you think peoples first impressions of you are?

....

....

....

....

....

RATING 💩💩💩💩💩

DATE: ....

NAME: ....

REASON FOR VISIT: ....

Q What is one opportunity you feel you missed out on?

....
....
....
....
....

RATING 💩💩💩💩💩

DATE: ....

NAME: ....

REASON FOR VISIT: ....

Q Who has had the greatest impact on you?

....
....
....
....
....

RATING 🧻🧻🧻🧻🧻

DATE: ....

NAME: ....

REASON FOR VISIT: ....

Q What traits do you get from your Mother/Father?

....
....
....
....
....

RATING 🧻🧻🧻🧻🧻

DATE: ....

NAME: ....

REASON FOR VISIT: ....

Q Who is one person you secretly envy and why?

....
....
....
....
....

RATING 💩💩💩💩💩

DATE: ....

NAME: ....

REASON FOR VISIT: ....

Q What series do you recommend to watch and why? ....

....

....

....

....

....

RATING 💩 💩 💩 💩 💩

DATE: ....

NAME: ....

REASON FOR VISIT: ....

Q What is the funniest joke you know by heart? ....

....

....

....

....

....

RATING 🧻 🧻 🧻 🧻 🧻

DATE: ....

NAME: ....

REASON FOR VISIT: ....

Q What do you love about your job & what do you hate? ....

....

....

....

....

....

RATING 🧻 🧻 🧻 🧻 🧻

DATE: ....

NAME: ....

REASON FOR VISIT: ....

Q How would you describe your relationship with your Mother? ....

....

....

....

....

....

RATING 💩 💩 💩 💩 💩

DATE: . . . .

NAME: . . . .

REASON FOR VISIT: . . . .

Q What are your 3 favorite sounds and why?

. . . .

. . . .

. . . .

. . . .

. . . .

RATING 💩 💩 💩 💩 💩

DATE: . . . .

NAME: . . . .

REASON FOR VISIT: . . . .

Q What recent memory makes you smile the most?

. . . .

. . . .

. . . .

. . . .

RATING 🧻 🧻 🧻 🧻 🧻

DATE: . . . .

NAME: . . . .

REASON FOR VISIT: . . . .

Q What story makes you cry with laughter every time you tell it? . . . .

. . . .

. . . .

. . . .

. . . .

RATING 🧻 🧻 🧻 🧻 🧻

DATE: . . . .

NAME: . . . .

REASON FOR VISIT: . . . .

Q If you were given $1500 right now and had to spend it in the next 12 hours, what would you spend it on? . .

. . . .

. . . .

. . . .

. . . .

RATING 💩 💩 💩 💩 💩

DATE: ....

NAME: ....

REASON FOR VISIT: ....

Q What animal would you be and why?
....

....

....

....

....

....

RATING 💩 💩 💩 💩 💩

DATE: ....

NAME: ....

REASON FOR VISIT: ....

Q What would you do if you had 2 hours to spare everyday?
....

....

....

....

....

....

RATING 🧻 🧻 🧻 🧻 🧻

DATE: ....

NAME: ....

REASON FOR VISIT: ....

Q What is the best Disney movie and why?
....

....

....

....

....

....

RATING 🧻 🧻 🧻 🧻 🧻

DATE: ....

NAME: ....

REASON FOR VISIT: ....

Q What film have you watched more than 3 times, why?
....

....

....

....

....

....

RATING 💩 💩 💩 💩 💩

DATE: ....

NAME: ....

REASON FOR VISIT: ....

Q What are your favorite smells and what do they remind you of? ....

....

....

....

....

....

....

RATING 💩 💩 💩 💩 💩

DATE: ....

NAME: ....

REASON FOR VISIT: ....

Q What is the last thing that made you LOL ? ....

....

....

....

....

....

....

RATING 🧻 🧻 🧻 🧻 🧻

DATE: ....

NAME: ....

REASON FOR VISIT: ....

Q Have you ever judged someone on their appearance and been totally wrong, who ? ....

....

....

....

....

....

....

RATING 🧻 🧻 🧻 🧻 🧻

DATE: ....

NAME: ....

REASON FOR VISIT: ....

Q What bad habits do you want to change or stop? ....

....

....

....

....

....

....

RATING 💩 💩 💩 💩 💩

DATE: ....

NAME: ....

REASON FOR VISIT: ....

Q Standing in front of heavens gates God asks you "Why should I let you in?" What do you say? ....

....
....
....
....
....
....

RATING 💩💩💩💩💩

DATE: ....

NAME: ....

REASON FOR VISIT: ....

Q What does your ideal morning look like?

....
....
....
....
....
....

RATING 🧻🧻🧻🧻🧻

DATE: ....

NAME: ....

REASON FOR VISIT: ....

Q If you had to start a business today, what would you do? ....

....
....
....
....
....
....

RATING 🧻🧻🧻🧻🧻

DATE: ....

NAME: ....

REASON FOR VISIT: ....

Q What job would you never ever do?

....
....
....
....
....
....

RATING 💩💩💩💩💩

DATE: ....

NAME: ....

REASON FOR VISIT: ....

Q What is your favorite place on earth?
....
....
....
....
....
....
....

RATING 💩💩💩💩💩

DATE: ....

NAME: ....

REASON FOR VISIT: ....

Q What is your favorite time of year and why?
....
....
....
....
....
....
....

RATING 🧻🧻🧻🧻🧻

DATE: ....

NAME: ....

REASON FOR VISIT: ....

Q What was the last dream you can remember?
....
....
....
....
....
....
....

RATING 🧻🧻🧻🧻🧻

DATE: ....

NAME: ....

REASON FOR VISIT: ....

Q What's the most interesting thing you've read or seen this week?
....
....
....
....
....
....
....

RATING 💩💩💩💩💩

DATE: ....
NAME: ....
REASON FOR VISIT: ....
Q What is one thing you wish you did earlier in life?
....
....
....
....
....
RATING 💩 💩 💩 💩 💩

DATE: ....
NAME: ....
REASON FOR VISIT: ....
Q What stresses you out the most?
....
....
....
....
....
RATING 🧻 🧻 🧻 🧻 🧻

DATE: ....
NAME: ....
REASON FOR VISIT: ....
Q What was the most memorable thing that happened last week?
....
....
....
....
....
RATING 🧻 🧻 🧻 🧻 🧻

DATE: ....
NAME: ....
REASON FOR VISIT: ....
Q What do you think about when you are driving?
....
....
....
....
....
RATING 💩 💩 💩 💩 💩

DATE: ....

NAME: ....

REASON FOR VISIT: ....

Q What's the most terrifying nightmare you have
ever had? ....

....

....

....

....

....

RATING 💩💩💩💩💩

DATE: ....

NAME: ....

REASON FOR VISIT: ....

Q Everyone has one book in them, what would yours be
about? ....

....

....

....

....

....

RATING 🧻🧻🧻🧻🧻

DATE: ....

NAME: ....

REASON FOR VISIT: ....

Q If you could make a documentary, what subject
would you choose and why? ....

....

....

....

....

....

RATING 🧻🧻🧻🧻🧻

DATE: ....

NAME: ....

REASON FOR VISIT: ....

Q If you didn't have to work, what would you be doing
with your time? ....

....

....

....

....

....

RATING 💩💩💩💩💩

DATE: ....

NAME: ....

REASON FOR VISIT: ....

Q When was the last time you felt lucky? ....

....

....

....

....

....

....

RATING 💩💩💩💩💩

DATE: ....

NAME: ....

REASON FOR VISIT: ....

Q What is the worst joke you know? ....

....

....

....

....

....

....

RATING 🧻🧻🧻🧻🧻

DATE: ....

NAME: ....

REASON FOR VISIT: ....

Q What was the worst decade for fashion and why? ...

....

....

....

....

....

....

RATING 🧻🧻🧻🧻🧻

DATE: ....

NAME: ....

REASON FOR VISIT: ....

Q Who was your favorite teacher and why? ....

....

....

....

....

....

....

RATING 💩💩💩💩💩

DATE: ....

NAME: ....

REASON FOR VISIT: ....

Q What animal would your Mother be and why? .....

....

....

....

....

....

RATING 💩 💩 💩 💩 💩

DATE: ....

NAME: ....

REASON FOR VISIT: ....

Q What would you do if you had a whole day to yourself but with no money to spend? ....

....

....

....

....

....

RATING 🧻 🧻 🧻 🧻 🧻

DATE: ....

NAME: ....

REASON FOR VISIT: ....

Q What is the best way to show someone you love them? .....

....

....

....

....

....

RATING 🧻 🧻 🧻 🧻 🧻

DATE: ....

NAME: ....

REASON FOR VISIT: ....

Q What song have you had on repeat for the last week, how does it make you feel? .....

....

....

....

....

....

RATING 💩 💩 💩 💩 💩

DATE: . . . .

NAME: . . . .

REASON FOR VISIT: . . . .

Q Was Michael Jackson innocent or guilty? Explain

. . . .

. . . .

. . . .

. . . .

. . . .

RATING 💩💩💩💩💩

DATE: . . . .

NAME: . . . .

REASON FOR VISIT: . . . .

Q What could modern society do without?

. . . .

. . . .

. . . .

. . . .

. . . .

RATING 🧻🧻🧻🧻🧻

DATE: . . . .

NAME: . . . .

REASON FOR VISIT: . . . .

Q Has social media improved the world?

. . . .

. . . .

. . . .

. . . .

. . . .

RATING 🧻🧻🧻🧻🧻

DATE: . . . .

NAME: . . . .

REASON FOR VISIT: . . . .

Q Biggie or Tupac? Explain

. . . .

. . . .

. . . .

. . . .

. . . .

RATING 💩💩💩💩💩

DATE: ....

NAME: ....

REASON FOR VISIT: ....

Q Where do you spend your most time online? ....

....

....

....

....

....

....

RATING 💩 💩 💩 💩 💩

DATE: ....

NAME: ....

REASON FOR VISIT: ....

Q Do you think going to college or university is better than getting a low paid job in your chosen field? .....

....

....

....

....

....

....

RATING 🧻 🧻 🧻 🧻 🧻

DATE: ....

NAME: ....

REASON FOR VISIT: ....

Q If you could have any plastic surgery for free, would you have anything done, if so, what and why? ....

....

....

....

....

....

....

RATING 🧻 🧻 🧻 🧻 🧻

DATE: ....

NAME: ....

REASON FOR VISIT: ....

Q What talent do you wish you had naturally? What would you do with said talent? ....

....

....

....

....

....

....

RATING 💩 💩 💩 💩 💩